Deconstruction of Self

Untangling Negative Thoughts About Yourself To Rebuild A Self Of Steel

By Landon T. Smith

I0438470

Table of Contents

Introduction

Suppose that you have a neighbor who always follows you around. This neighbor criticizes you for your actions, tells you lies about yourself and tries to take credit away from any accomplishment that you make. How would you feel about that person? If you're like most people, you've been frustrated with this bad neighbor and you'd do everything in your power to kick him to the curb. Maybe you'd lock him out of your car, tell him to go away, even call the police. Most of us wouldn't tolerate bullying from someone else, especially if it were 24/7.

But then, let's change the scenario. Let's imagine that this isn't a neighbor at all, but was rather a simple voice within your head. How differently would you treat that voice? When you accomplish something, that voice tells you how you're wrong. If you do something well, the voice will tell you it wasn't enough. The voice will always try to take away your joy and happiness away. What do you do about that voice?

Here's where the tough truth comes in: we usually listen to this voice as if it were true. When the voice says "you're not good enough," you sullenly nod your head, knowing that ultimately whatever this voice says is the truth. Since it's coming from your own mind, why wouldn't it be true? And then, you find that you have a problem that everyone else in the world suffers from as well, you are dealing with a negative thought life that is poisoning you and taking away your happiness.

That's the problem when it comes to negative thoughts. The way we think indicates how we live, not the other way around. This is why we see people who are living outwardly successful lives end up so depressed. You can have a gorgeous spouse, a big house, lots of money and success, but if your inward life is miserable, then it won't do you any good. You will rot from the inside.

So how many of us are currently rotting from the inside due to this constant stream of negativity? I would wager to say that most of the world deals with this Inner Critic, a person who relentlessly tells us negative things and seeks to punish us for the simple act of trying to find happiness.

While this might be a bleak summary, we do have some good news: you don't always have to live that way. You don't have to let this negative voice, this inner critic rule over your life anymore. In fact, you have the power to change your life by embarking on a deconstruction of yourself, where you are willing to take apart your thought processes and ask yourself "why?" No matter how old you are, you didn't reach this kind of thought process overnight. You didn't wake up one morning to discover that there is a negative voice, telling you that you can't do anything right. This voice grows over time and is reflective of the thoughts and information that have been put inside of us from a very early age.

The purpose of this book is to help you unleash the power of deconstruction, teaching you how to overcome that negative voice in your head by going down deep into the roots of your being and finding out what fills your mind. It's never an easy process when you decide to get past the negativity, but with the help of this book and a willingness to look within your own mind, you will find that it is indeed possible to overcome the darkness within. You can heal your internal world so that regardless of the external circumstances that you have, you will be full of happiness and joy. If you're ready to get to work, head over to the next chapter, where we will look at the question of how to approach deconstruction in a healthy manner.

Chapter 1: Tearing up the Foundation

Now, we must look at the concept of deconstruction in terms of a building, in order to better understand it. When a house has a major problem with it, for example, it could have a weak foundation that is unable to support the weight, there is very little that can be done outside of fixing the foundation. However, to repair a foundation is quite the endeavor, as the foundation is the very base of a building itself. Without the foundation, the building will collapse. Yet, if the foundation isn't properly built, it could weaken the house to the point where the house is unable to endure heavy winds or bad storms. Perhaps it couldn't even support the weight necessary in order to make the house large and luxurious.

Very few people would argue that the best way to fix a bad foundation is to make simple adjustments to the aesthetic of the house. You'd consider a man insane if he told you that his house could collapse due to a faulty foundation and his plan to handle it was to put a nice rug on the ground. That would have little to no effect. Now, let's think about how we think as a foundation in itself. Our thoughts, our beliefs, our ideas are all part of the foundation of how our mind works. When we suffer from negative thoughts and ideas, we are often tempted to try and remove the negative thoughts.

For example, if someone is dealing with anxiety and they consistently worry that other people do not like them, they might say to themselves "Stop worrying" as a method of fixing the problem. This, of course, does very little other than make the anxious person feel guilty about how they feel. This is about on par with the man who throws the rug on the ground and declares the foundation issue to be fixed.

There are plenty of symptoms when it comes to a faulty foundation in a house. Floors are sloping about, bricks in the walls are cracking due to the strain, the walls are warping a little. All of these are nothing more than *indicators* of an actual problem. If you were to try and fix the bricks, or push the walls back, it still isn't fixing the problem. It's the same when it comes to our inner thought life. A faulty mental foundation has plenty of symptoms, depression, anxiety, anger, fear, worry, etc. All of these things tend to manifest into an inner voice that can't want to make us feel bad about ourselves. If we were to make the mistake of believing that the symptoms were the problem, we would spend a great deal of time distracting ourselves with things that cannot be fixed until the foundation has been examined.

Suppose that you are constantly dealing with negative thinking, your inner voice is very strong and also very unhelpful to you. It criticizes, complains and tells you that you aren't good enough. If you spend all of your time focusing on figuring out some way to silence the voice, you most likely will grow frustrated with the inability to stop it. That is because you are simply focusing on a symptom. The real solution to all of these deeper emotional and psychological issues is to look at our foundation.

So what is the foundation of our mind? What is the foundation of our thinking? If we were to sum it up in a single word, we would say belief. A belief is a preconceived notion about how the world is and how it is supposed to be. Our beliefs are formed at a very early age and are shaped throughout our lives. It is quite an intricate and complex process as to how beliefs are formed, but these are the central pieces of our minds. Everything that we think moves through what we believe.

And this is where the problem lies, because a belief doesn't necessarily have to line up with reality. So a man can believe that he can fly, he can truly believe it in his heart of hearts, but when he leaps off a building flapping his arms like wings, regardless of what he thinks, reality will inform him differently. And this is the problem that we ourselves get stuck in, because our beliefs color everything that we do, so much so that they dictate how we act, regardless of what the reality is. In certain cases, it can be extremely damaging, such as the anorexic who has a belief that she is fat, when in reality she is very skinny and not eating would do more harm than good.

So, if beliefs are our foundation when it comes to understanding the way we think, it means that we must be able to learn how to change our beliefs in order to live a better life. However, this is not an easy act in the slightest. Just as rebuilding a foundation requires a lot of time, effort and energy, so does rebuilding a belief. But, let's not get ahead of ourselves. We must first come to truly acknowledge that our beliefs have a major role in the way we think, then we must look to how beliefs are formed and shaped, so that we can have mastery over them.

It's never easy when it comes to learning how to change our beliefs. The default nature of the human brain is to stay the way it is and resist change at all costs. It's part of our DNA, we're wired to want to keep our minds in the exact same state so that we are able to readily and easily identify danger. There can be a tremendous pain when it comes to changing the way we think. So before we start digging into how we can change, let's dig into the question of why our brains work the way they do in regards to beliefs.

The first thing to understand about a belief is the fact that our brains are designed from a very early age to absorb a lot of information. As we grow, we begin to perceive and experience a great deal of data that has an impact on how we live our lives. For example, when a baby cries loudly and receives a bottle, it will learn that it has the power to summon food by crying out loudly. If every time the baby cries, he receives a bottle, his brain will come to the conclusion that this is the most effective way to get food.

Things change, as the baby grows though, and soon he isn't given food when he cries. Does this change his behaviors? No. He will continue to cry for food, as he was trained this way. Some parents discover there are other methods to stop the child from crying, by giving him a pacifier or distracting him with a toy, but there will be a basic pattern ingrained into his mind that when he cries, he gets food.

The brain looks for patterns as a way to store information and come to conclusions. This is how the brain looks at the world around it. Concepts like shapes, colors, tastes, all stay relatively consistent within our brains because of these patterns. For example, every ball in the world is round. Why is that? Because that is the pattern that we have learned. We would never look at a square shaped object and believe it to be a ball, because our brains have learned that there is only one type of ball and that is a round one.

What are the purposes of these patterns? Well, for one, it's how we store information into our memories. The more important a pattern is to you, the more your brain learns to keep that information handy. For example, if you touched a stove when you were little, it probably burned you pretty bad. That created a powerful neural pathway that informed your brain that touching an active stove is bad for you. When we see a busy street full of traffic, our brain kindly reminds us that it is a terrible idea to go rushing into traffic because of what cars can do to the human body.

So the brain, from the very beginning, is an information storing machine. It absorbs any information that is placed in it, regardless of whether that information is true or not. The brain doesn't have the ability to filter at an early age, primarily because we don't have our reasoning skills developed enough to protect us from bad thoughts. For example, if you were to tell a three year old that a car was called a spoon, he would have no ability to disagree with you until he grew up and developed the logic and reasoning skills to contradict you.

This storage of information poses a unique problem to us, however. As the brain works to keep information tightly controlled, we do encounter new information that contradicts old information. When the brain is young and malleable, it easily adapts to this new information. When the new information does not conflict with strong beliefs, we usually adapt pretty well. However, when information contradicts a belief, the belief will always win.

So how do beliefs form? Well, as we are growing up, we begin to develop an understanding of self and how the self relates to the world. We are told information by people that we trust, either teachers or parents, and these things stick in deeply. A parent who tells their son that he is very smart, will begin to develop a belief that he is an intelligent child. However, things can tend to awry when emotion comes into the mix.

Emotion is the anti-rational part of the human experience. Emotion makes life worth living, but can also have a devastating effect on the human mind. Things like happiness are wonderful and the human brains wants as much of it as it can get, but things like fear can lead the brain to develop patterns to avoid dealing with fear.

As we are growing up, we have certain interactions that deliver a powerful negative emotion to our brains. These are moments where we are told something negative, we experience something bad or become ashamed of ourselves. Our brain learns from that experience and looks at that painful moment as something to avoid at all costs. Like when our fingers touched the burner and discovered how bad of an idea it was, so the brain learns that certain emotional trauma must be avoided at all cost.

This is where negative beliefs begin to form. A negative emotional event will convince the brain that something about you is true, and in your early age, you have no ability to deny that. You cannot use reason, you cannot use logic, you are entirely at the mercy of your emotional center which has told you something negative about yourself.

And so we see the deep roots of our negative self-image begin to form. The most powerful of all of these negative parts of our minds is what we call shame. Shame informs us that we aren't enough the way we are, it tells us that we are bad people and that we should feel bad for our choices. When our parents use shame to motivate and control us, it creates deep wounds that shape our beliefs. The human mind isn't equipped to deal with shame, because we develop this sense at such an early age. So by the time we're old enough to reason effectively, in our teen years and older, we have already have a strong foundation of shame.

Where does shame come from, exactly? Well, it comes from those negative emotional events that make you feel bad about yourself. Perhaps you were rejected socially when you were very young, maybe someone was abusive to you, maybe you did something wrong and were told that you were a bad person because of what you did. Shame sinks down to the core of our hearts and begins to shape the beliefs that we have. The brain develops methods of trying to protect itself from those feelings of shame and creates impulses designed to protect.

Let's create a picture of what this looks like. If a four year old wants to play with his father, but his father is too busy to pay any attention to his boy, he will persist in trying to get his dad's attention. The father becomes angry with his son and punishes him for being "annoying" and a feeling of shame envelops the child's mind. He begins to feel shame and his mind becomes acutely aware of how bad that shame is. The brain, looking for patterns, then tries to piece together why the boy is feeling this kind of pain. The brain, using only the information that it has, comes to the conclusion that trying to get his father's attention was what caused the shame. It then creates a belief that he must be quiet in order to avoid the pain of being shamed again.

This child grows up with a fundamental belief that it is safer to be seen and not heard, then consistently struggles for the rest of his life with being outspoken, extroverted or outgoing. Now, as he develops, he grows in his reasoning skills and learns how to control his mind to the point where he is now master over his brain. The brain no longer makes the decisions on an automatic level, but the boy makes his own choices on a very conscious level. So he chooses to spend time with his friends, to curry favor from a woman, to be heard as well as seen.

But something is nagging away at the man's mind. When he gets home, the voice within his mind begins to tell him of all the things that he did wrong. He feels ashamed of himself and fears that his friends found him to be annoying or overbearing. These thoughts are compulsive and he cannot rid himself of these feelings, no matter how hard he tries to think them away or counter them with rationality.

The reason he has these irrational thoughts is that even though he has control over his conscious mind, it is his subconscious mind that is fueling those feelings and negative thoughts. The unconscious mind still very truly believes that it is better to be seen and not heard, and regardless of whatever this man learns, until the belief is tackled, he will never overcome those thoughts.

This is the core problem when it comes to learning how to change our minds. Our minds are fiercely protective of ourselves and look at these traumatic events as something to avoid at all costs. So, if we were to try and change our own minds, we would find fierce resistance, for the brain wants to stay the same so that it is able to survive.

This explains why it can be so distressing when we begin to look inward to our own emotional hang-ups and learn to discern the problems that are within us. Most of the time, our brain isn't keen to this because it involves changing information that has been settled down for a very long time. It requires examining old beliefs and making new ones, something the mind isn't super well equipped for. And of course, the older we get, the more painful this process becomes. But, don't be dismayed because it is possible to change the way we think, it is possible to uproot broken beliefs and find new, healthier ones, but it takes work. Let's move on to the next chapter where we will examine how to investigate our unhealthy beliefs and how they are interacting with us right now.

Chapter 2: Belief Problems

So we've made the case for why beliefs are the root of our emotional and psychological unhealthiness. It's fairly clear that the culprit lies in how we were raised, but that isn't the only part of the problem. There is also another issue that must clearly be addressed: reinforcement. Remember, the brain works to identify patterns, each time it sees something as part of the same pattern, it gets stronger. We would call this reinforcement. A single event can have a major impact on your life and the initial belief begins to form, but the belief doesn't take full control of you yet. The belief, being in infancy, still requires a lot of reinforcement in order to grow stronger.

Here's the problem then, once the belief forms, it becomes a lens, *everything that happens to you is seen through those lenses*. This means that your belief begins to look for ways to validate itself. Each time it finds a way to validate itself, it grows a little stronger, until eventually it is firmly rooted within your mind. What does this mean for us? Well, to put it lightly, it means that our perception itself is shaped by our beliefs, almost to the point where we are constantly looking to confirm our belief. This is why there are certain types of people in this world who can be offended at the most innocuous things, they are actually looking for something to be offended at. The same goes for our belief structures, we are looking to have our beliefs confirmed.

This creates what is known as a confirmation bias. Confirmation bias is one of the most prevalent parts of the human experience. Think about how ideologies work differently from one another. If someone who was pro-war read an article about the War in Iraq, they would come away with an entirely different opinion than someone who was anti-war, despite the fact that they read the exact same article. Confirmation bias is basically our brains way of looking to confirm information that it already believes. This only strengthens the belief. And since we live in a culture where our deep rooted negative beliefs aren't being challenged, they only grow stronger and stronger. Then they become a dominating factor in our lives and we wonder how we will ever begin to recover from such a pain.

So let's start moving away from the theoretical realm to the personal realm instead. This book isn't just about developmental psychology, rather it is all about figuring out how to help you change up that negative thought pattern in your mind that has been preventing you from living a happy and healthy life. So let's look at what the first step is in this process of deconstruction: examination.

Examination is the process of being able to look at every aspect of your life and ask yourself questions to understand where your thought processes are coming from. Unfortunately, our modern culture is very surface level and is highly focused on finding external answers instead of internal ones. For example, if someone is in a bad mood and they are feeling very angry but aren't sure why, they might be tempted to blame the weather or something they ate for their frustration. Those things are external circumstances and hold very little affect on us, but we can believe erroneously that external factors are responsible for our thoughts and emotions.

This leads us into falling into the trap known as Life Enhancement. This philosophy believes that the best way to fix your problems is to change the circumstances around you. So instead of digging into the unresolved emotional tension and pain inside of your heart, you try to get a new job, or you look for a new car. There are no external solutions to internal problems, and most of our emotional problems are very internalized. Yes, there are those who are struggling with legitimate chemical imbalances that are causing their emotional disorders, but there are a great many of us who actually have perfectly healthy brains and unhealthy beliefs. Unless you have been diagnosed professionally, there is a very high chance that your emotional issues are internal, not external.

So how do we begin to examine ourselves? Well, it starts with recording your own negative thoughts until you are able to identify a pattern. The negative voice within our minds all take different shapes and communicate different things to us. No two voices are alike, some are highly critical of how you look, others could be critical of what you wear and so on and so forth.

Being able to identify what your negative voice is telling you will be extremely crucial when it comes to digging in deeper. So let's go ahead and break this examination processes down step by step.

Examination Step One: Identify your Inner Critic

We'll call this negative voice the Inner Critic, as that is a somewhat popular term in the modern world. This Inner Critic interacts with everyone differently, so it's important that you are able to put a list of attributes and qualities to your Inner Critic, so that you can identify what the patterns are. Remember, the brain works entirely off of patterns, they are the building blocks of human thought, so we cannot assume that each thought is merely an isolated instance.

So it starts with a simple awareness exercise. Stop for a moment and think about your own thoughts. This is kind of a weird thing to think about, but you must realize that the miracle of human consciousness allows us to think about the thoughts we are currently having. This is what is referred to as "meta-thinking" and it allows us to understand what is going on in your mind on a deeper level.

So stop and just think about your thoughts. What is coming to your mind? What emotions, what memories? What ideas? Now, begin to think about the constant nagging sensation that you have, whatever this unpleasant voice is within your mind, what does it say to you? Does it speak in words or does it replay sharply unpleasant memories? What is the pattern here? Get into the habit of simply thinking about the negative thoughts that come up. Start to see if you can identify what those thoughts are. Oftentimes we have such powerful negative thoughts, but we completely let them move through us automatically, never bothering to think about the thought itself. By actively stopping to identify what your Inner Critic is saying, you'll have a better chance of understanding how to interact with it.

Examination Step Two: Catch the Negative Thought

The next step, after you've started to get into the habit of actively listening to what your negative voice is saying, is to get into the habit of catching your negative thoughts and holding onto them. The purpose of this isn't to stop them from happening, you're not trying to grab thoughts out of thin air and make them go away, instead, you're going to want to try and follow your negative thoughts a little more.

For example, let's suppose that you are walking down the street and a negative thought comes to you and says "You're worthless and an idiot," instead of arguing with that voice, agreeing with it or ignoring it, try stopping your thinking entirely and focus only on that impulse. Start to ask yourself, where did this come from? Ask if it belongs there or not. Start to trace where this thought is coming from. You'll discover something interesting at this point, you'll discover that these negative thoughts don't exist in a vacuum. They are actually linked to something happening in your mind right now which takes us to our third step.

Examination Step Three: Follow the Emotion

Our negative thoughts are usually highly connected to our emotions, but a lot of times we can ignore those emotions that we are feeling for fear that they aren't particularly healthy. Let's use the example from the previous step, if you have a thought tell you that you are worthless, you are also feeling an emotion that is indicating that as well. What does this emotion mean, however? Is it sorrow, shame, sadness? These things don't come out of nowhere, but rather they are a part of our emotional core. So grab onto the negative thought and then begin to follow the emotion.

What do I mean by following the emotion? I mean, try to trace the origination of the emotion within you. This means you should ask questions like "what caused this shift in me?" or "what was I just thinking about?" A lot of these negative emotions are powerful sources of discomfort that can lead us to try and avoid thinking about them, but the truth is that we must be willing to dig into our negative emotions so that we can figure out where they are coming from. We call this process "emotional forensics' because it assumes that there is always a root cause to our emotions.

It is these root emotions that are triggering the negative thoughts, because the negative thoughts are a *response* to our beliefs. So let's look at the timeline of how things happen in our brains. First, there is some kind of triggering response, our emotions kick in and our beliefs then begin to create thoughts based on those emotions. If we believe that a certain emotion is bad, the belief will try to provide information to our brains to avoid that particular trigger. So, if we are feeling bad about ourselves, it's actually some kind of coping mechanism designed to prevent us from feeling an even higher level of pain on some level.

Of course, this is paradoxical because the coping mechanism also makes us feel terrible. In a lot of ways, this process is like an emotional fever. The purpose of the physical fever is to kill an infection and protect the body, but if a fever gets too strong, it can actually kill the very person it is trying to protect. This is how our brain operates, sans any kind of special training. By default, this is a highly ineffective system and condemns us to living a life of negative thoughts and misery.

Examination Step Four: Identify Core Beliefs

This is probably one of the harder parts of the examination process. Once you've learned how to investigate your negative voices and use the emotional forensic process to identify the emotional cores that are fueling your discomfort and negative feelings, you must then figure out what your core beliefs are. This is never an easy process, because there are a lot of false things that can get in our way when it comes to identifying beliefs. We are often looking for a simple and easy explanation for why we act the way we do, so we often like to point to disorders as being the problem.

"I'm just depressed," says a man who has been struggling with a toxic, violent voice inside of him for all of his life. "And that's my problem." The problem here is that the depression is a *symptom* not the problem. It is the symptom of a negative core belief about himself that is leading him to feel very oppressed. This isn't to say that his feelings and thoughts are lies, or that he is faking his pain, all of those things are very real. But the root isn't some psychological disorder, the root is in his negative beliefs.

So how do we go about identifying our core beliefs? Well, we must start from the outside and work out way in. It starts with following a negative thought all the way down to the emotional experiences that formed that belief. So, let's try to break it down into a series of steps so you don't get lost along the way.

Step One: Identify the negative thought

This is an easy one, we've already discussed it. It starts with becoming aware of a negative thought in your mind instead of ignoring it or agreeing with it.

Step Two: Follow the negative thought to the emotion that began to produce it

Once you've identified the negative thought, try to think about how that thought makes you feel. These feelings are actually the root source of the negative thought, but the thought is the more visible of the two. Once you have a clear identification of how you feel, you must then dig deeper.

Step Three: Ask where the emotion itself is coming from.

You must then turn your attention to the question: where is this emotion itself coming from? Emotions are powerful things, but they don't show up uninvited. Something on some level has triggered these emotions. This isn't an easy thing to examine and will most likely take a lot of introspective and thinking about your memories.

Step Four: Look for common patterns between these negative thoughts

Over time, you will find that these negative thoughts have some kind of pattern to them, the pattern is either in what they are telling you or how they are making you feel. For example, a pattern could make you feel like you are worthless or the pattern could tell you that you can never achieve anything. Once you have a firm understanding of what these patterns are, you can then progress into investigating the root of these patterns.

Step Five: Ask yourself, what is the root of these patterns

You must have a willingness to go past surface explanations of your problems and instead ask what is the root of these patterns. Don't blame external things. Instead, try to ask yourself, where did this start? This isn't an easy thing to do because it requires you to have the willingness to look back into your past, to the early years of your development and look for the things that have caused you so much pain.

In other words, you must be willing to visit the traumas and pains that happened at an early age, because these traumas will dictate how your emotional life will function throughout your life. You probably know when these negative things happened, you just might not have sorted through them, or worse, since you were just a child, you might have simply believed these traumatic things to indicate how reality works.

For example, if you have noticed that your negative patterns are always based around shame and feelings of inadequacy, you could spend time digging into your past and asking, "when was the first time I felt this way?" In the process of asking that question, you could discover that you felt that way when your father told you that you were worthless because of something that you did wrong.

This kind of process takes time and can be difficult to do alone, primarily because once you begin to look back, it will start to open up a flood of raw and primal emotions that you might not feel equipped to handle. But the good news is that you are very equipped to handle these feelings, because these feelings aren't current, they are just *memories*. Memories do not have the power to harm you any further, but you have the power to heal from them. But in order to heal from them, you must be able to first know where these root problems are coming from. This isn't going to happen overnight, it will take time, contemplation and a willingness to dig into your own psyche.

Step Six: Look for more instances where this core negative experience happened.

Once you've gotten an understanding of what the core negative experience is, you can then go about the process of looking for other instances where this negative experience was reinforced. For example, if you are dealing with a powerful memory of being told that you were worthless, you can probably pinpoint a few more times in your life where you felt that way from an early age. Each instance strengthens your brains conclusion that you are worthless and confirms the belief. Being able to see how many times this experience occurs in your life will give you an understanding as to the strength and significance of this negative belief.

This process also allows you to find the difference between a bad memory and a memory that shaped your beliefs. Everyone has bad memories of something that caused them pain, but were able to live their lives without it affecting them at all. We're looking for the deep scars that wounded you for your entire life. If you find there is a particularly painful emotional moment, but it doesn't seem to create any patterns in your memories where you were constantly reliving that experience, then it most likely didn't form a negative belief or you were able to get through it without being negatively affected.

After you've gone through these steps enough to identify a core experience that has affected you and you can see how it has dictated thoughts and emotions throughout your life, you are done with the examination phase. This stage is extremely crucial and takes time. Don't be in a rush to figure out what your negative beliefs are, chances are they are rooted in very deeply. The process of figuring out where those beliefs are coming from and how the trauma in your life has led you to these conclusions can be very painful.

One side effect of having to look at trauma and negative thoughts head on is the fact that it might create an overwhelming feeling of despair and pain in your heart. This is the nature of change, however. Do not be dismayed if you feel like it hurts too bad to keep on going, that is simply your brain trying to prevent you from changing. Remember, the brain doesn't like changing anything because it wants to protect you. This leads it to create strong emotions as you go about trying to grow and it can discourage you if you aren't ready for it. If you want to change your beliefs, you must be ready for the pain and the feelings of being destroyed. Those feelings aren't true, however, you aren't being destroyed, you are being rebuilt.

Which leads us to our next chapter: Rebuilding the Broken Belief.

Chapter 3: Tearing Down Before You Build Up

By this point, you may have an inkling of what your negative beliefs are and you are hoping to change them. You might be looking forward to living a life free of that inner critic that has condemned you to live such a life of unhappiness. You might be ready to just start cramming in positive thoughts to counteract the negative thoughts, but let's not get too ahead of ourselves.

If we keep the metaphor of how changing our beliefs is like repairing a foundation, we must recognize that there is a process of examination and repair, but before you can repair a foundation, you must be willing to tear the bad parts out. This tearing process is painful but is ultimately necessary.

This chapter is all about learning how to tear down your negative beliefs once you have identified them. This involves a process of being able to challenge yourself and your own thinking so that you are able to make changes. Don't make the mistake of thinking that all you need to do is drop a few positive beliefs on top of your negative ones in order to cure them, instead, you must be willing to learn the process of challenging yourself so that you can effectively work to eradicate old beliefs while simultaneously building new beliefs.

This is a complicated process, but we'll break it down one piece at a time for you. The most crucial process of deconstruction is learning how to challenge yourself. That is the crux here, if you can challenge your own beliefs, you will get out of this well. So let's look at a series of steps and strategies that can help you understand how to challenge your own negative beliefs.

Challenge Step One: Asking Why

The first real way to challenge any kind of information is to simply ask why. Why do you believe that? Hopefully, during your examination time, you should be able to identify what your belief is, but now it is time to ask why do you believe it now? You might not have an answer right away, because with a deeply ingrained belief, it probably feels natural to you. So if I were to say "why do you feel worthless?" You might say "I don't know," or "just because." Both of these answers are unsatisfactory because they are *deflections* from the question. The question is why. Until you are able to answer why, you won't be able to progress into changing your old beliefs into new ones.

You should be able to figure out why after some time of thinking and chewing on the question. You might have come up with a few answers already. Once you have your answer figured out, it's time to move onto the next step.

Challenge Step Two: Is that a Valid Reason?

You must then go about the process of looking at that belief and asking yourself if it is a valid reason to have that belief. For example, sticking with the worthlessness feelings, if your answer to the question of why was "because my dad told me that I would be," you must then ask yourself if that is a valid reason for why your belief is true.

And here is where we find the tension between fantasy and reality. You see, a belief can exist independent of reality. So we bring a lot of invalid and faulty reasoning into the equation in order to justify a belief that has no business existing. There are three sides to any story, your side, their side and the truth. The truth operates independently of whatever your belief is. So we find ourselves in a struggle between reality and the internal construct of our own mind. And the problem is that when you believe something is true, there is no amount of external input that can convince you that the information is false. You and you alone are the only one who has the power to change your mind. So the reason we ask, "is that a valid reason?" is because to you, the answer will always be yes. If that belief didn't have a valid (in your own mind) reason, then it wouldn't exist as firmly as it did which leads to the next part of the process.

Challenge Step Three: Examine your Justifications

Since the brain developed a belief structure, it also develops justifications to keep those beliefs alive. These justifications are often deeply rooted in our minds and allow our beliefs to exist unchallenged. You are the only person who is able to examine the justifications that you use to keep a negative belief alive. This is a hard thing to swallow, because in a lot of ways, you are doing things to keep these negative beliefs fully functional and operational. Of course, we're not saying that you want to be miserable or you want to have an inner critic, but your habits and mindset up until now has led to the creation of a very powerful negative thought life. This didn't happen without your permission.

Justifications are the things we use to keep our negative beliefs. We would also use the word "excuses" in place of justification. Of course, excuse isn't a term I prefer mainly because the word causes defensiveness in us. No one wants to be accused of giving excuses, but let's try to step away from the emotional context of the word and focus on the reason why you have justified the existence of your belief.

At the end of the day, your negative belief is somehow protecting you. It is keeping you safe from something and the brain has given you a great incentive to keep that belief. In addition, the belief has become a habit of yours, that way of thinking is now automatic and we are used to it. We, as humans, love comfort above all else and will do anything we can to stay in our area of comfort. Challenging a negative belief is uncomfortable, so we develop justifications so that we can stay in our comfort zone.

So what kind of justifications do you have? Here's a simple list of the different types of justifications that can be used to explain away why we're holding onto our negative belief.

I am Statements: An I Am statement changes our behavior to a state of being. For example, a woman might say "I am ashamed of myself" instead of saying "I feel ashamed." These kinds of statements justify the existence of a negative belief because the person is saying that their belief is a part of their identity. That would be like saying I am a lampshade instead of saying I have a lampshade. This is a big difference. The brain listens intently to self-talk. The way you communicate to your own self will dictate how your brain will interact with its beliefs. The more you reinforce a negative belief by claiming it is a part of you, the harder it will be to change.

Dismissals: A dismissal is simply telling yourself and others that your negative beliefs aren't a big deal or they aren't real problems. Some people might say things like "Well, at least I wasn't beaten as a child." Truthfully, this is nothing more than a dismissal of your own experiences and your own feelings. When we dismiss our trauma and problems, we are telling ourselves that our belief isn't a big deal. This allows the belief to continue profoundly affecting the way you live, without you having a chance of uprooting it.

Pride: Strange as it may be, there has been a trend in recent years of seeing people develop a certain amount of pride over their negative traits. Some people have chosen to give up on finding healing and transformation and instead allow themselves to be classified and identified as "depressed" or "an introvert" or "socially incapable." The problem is that once you have begun to develop a sense of identity based around a negative belief, that belief will work its way into all of aspects of your life. In other words, the more attention you give to acquiescing to a negative belief instead of challenging it, the more powerful it will become.

Challenge Step Four: Dismantle your Justifications

This is the final step when it comes to challenging yourself and it's certainly the hardest one. You must be willing to take a look at the justifications that you have been using to keep your negative beliefs reinforced and you must be willing to give them up. This won't remove your negative belief, however, but it will loosen it up enough for you to be able to pave over it with positive beliefs. If you don't dismantle your justifications, if you aren't able to counter and overcome the self-destructive things that you are thinking to yourself, you will never be free of your negative beliefs.

This is easier said than done. Once you have been able to identify what your justifications have been, you must be willing to change your relationship to your justifications. Instead of saying "this is just how I am," make a conscious effort to say "this is something that I do." Instead of telling people "I'm depressed," change your language to say "I struggle with feelings of depression." This might seem small at first, but by learning how to separate your thoughts from your state of being, you will be able to weaken your beliefs. Remember, your beliefs are about *who you are*. These negative thoughts are entirely about your identity and your sense of self. If you are able to separate your identity from the thoughts and emotions that you are having, your brain won't nearly be as defensive when it come to finally changing.

Ultimately, the process of being able to consistently look at your own beliefs and challenge their existence is integral to the reconstruction process; however, that is not the end of it. If we want to change a belief for good, we must develop a new and more positive belief in order to be able to function properly. The brain isn't equipped to not think about things, so there is really no way for you to simply "stop" when it comes to thinking and believing in a certain way. Instead, we must learn how to replace them with positive beliefs.

As stated before, however, these positive beliefs must be brought in after you have challenged your old beliefs enough to the point where you feel ready to overcome them. When you do feel ready, move over to the next chapter and begin.

Chapter 4: Positive Changes in Your Head

So now we finally come to the point where we shall look at how to make overwhelmingly positive changes in your mind. This involves learning how to adapt to new beliefs and letting those things run your life. This will ultimately lessen the power of the Inner Critic and in some cases, cause the Inner Critic to cease existing entirely. Now, that is well worth it!

So let's talk about what it means to change a belief first. As mentioned in the last chapter, we can't really remove our beliefs. This is because the brain doesn't have the ability to not think about something. For example, if I were to say, don't think about a pink elephant, you would have no choice but to think of a pink elephant. No matter how hard you tried, your brain would be forced to think about it.

When it comes to changing our beliefs, we often try to stop believing a negative belief, but that doesn't do us any good. Like the pink elephant, if we try to tell our brains "don't have that belief or don't think those thoughts" your brain will then only think about that. And to make it worse, the harder we try to not think about it, the more your brain will think about it. This leads to the paradox of the belief growing stronger and the negative talk getting louder.

So we're not here to remove beliefs entirely, instead we are here to transform them. If we can learn how to change the way we think and how we interact with our negative beliefs, we can develop a strong inner thought life and it will ultimately change the way we think. Negative beliefs do not vanish immediately, it can take years and years of effort to overcome.

There is, in modern culture, an urge to see a "breakthrough" that changes the way a person thinks instantaneously. This is usually portrayed in dramas and televisions as a big moment when a person is going through therapy, they have a sudden realization about themselves and everything changes in their life. This is a piece of fiction and isn't a realistic portrayal of what change looks like. Change is soft and slow, it's gradual. Radical changes are usually external changes, and those things don't help us when it comes to overcoming destructive beliefs. So don't be in a rush, it will take time. It will take effort.

With that in mind, let's go ahead and begin reviewing the different steps that you can take to start changing your negative beliefs.

Positive Belief Step One: Develop Perspective

Often times we find that we are stuck with only our own perspective of the world around us. For all of our lives, we are inside of our bodies, hearing words through our ears and looking out into the world through our eyes. Everything that we perceive moves through a powerful filter, that filter is our own perspective. No matter who you are, how wise you are or how much insight you have into the world, you will always have an extremely limited perspective about yourself.

This is problematic when it comes to developing a new positive belief because we don't have the ability to think outside of our own experiences.

Think about it like this, imagine that you were trying to navigate through the woods, but you had no idea where you were. You were lost and from your perspective, every place seems the exact same to you. Yet, if you were to get a bird's eye view of the forest, you'd know exactly where to go. The problem here is that the only way for us to be able to get a bird's eye view is to get perspective from people or things outside of ourselves.

That's right, if you were hoping to achieve enlightenment and freedom alone, then I'm sorry to say that just isn't the case. Our beliefs are deeply rooted and since they act as filters for how we perceive reality, we can't really trust ourselves. We have a very strong confirmation bias and that confirmation bias will sabotage our ability to get a better perspective. The easiest way to gain new perspectives about your personality, your beliefs and your problems is to look to someone who can provide you with their thoughts about the situation.

This might be a bit vulnerable, for it requires you to be honest about the Inner Critic and admit that things are less than ideal inside of your brain, but that's perfectly fine. It's natural for us to feel uncomfortable when talking about our innermost struggles, but if you can find the right person to share your feelings and thoughts with, you will find very valuable perspective. Now, it's important to make sure that you are selecting the right person for the job. Don't pick anyone, rather they should be a friend that you are close with and respect. Everyone has an opinion on everything and many people are in a rush to tell you how to live your life, so make sure that you present yourself not as someone looking for advice, but looking for a different perspective. Avoid the type of person who will tell you exactly what you need to do to fix your life, because those people tend to have messy lives themselves.

You also might want to consider using the services of a professional, such as a counselor, therapist or even a minister. These people are usually trained to listen and provide you with a good sounding board so that you are able to develop a greater perspective about your beliefs.

The more outside understanding that you have of your thought processes, the easier it is for you to begin to form newer ways of thinking.

Positive Belief Step Two: Figure out the Opposite of your negative belief

Once you have a greater level of perspective, you can then begin to figure out what the opposite of your negative belief is. Believe it or not, but the opposite of your negative belief isn't non-existence. Rather, it is a positive trait. Strap your helmet on here, because we are going deep into philosophical meanings of good and bad.

Oftentimes we perceive things as being bad simply because they are harmful to us and as such, we assume that the opposite of pain is absence of pain. Truthfully, the opposite of pain is the presence of pleasure, at least when it comes to our beliefs. The brain doesn't have the ability to operate in a neutral state because the process of being alive is a very active thing. We don't exist on a neutral spectrum, instead we are either sliding towards negativity or climbing our way up to positivity. This affects the way we develop personality traits and beliefs. In other words, the opposite of your negative belief is actually a positive belief that will help you succeed in your life and develop the kind of character that you want.

Even more interesting is the fact that most negative beliefs have positive counterparts that are closely related to each other. Remember, a negative belief formed because the brain was looking to protect you and as such, it was meant for good. The problem was that even though it was meant for good, it has disastrous effects on your mental health and general wellbeing. Think of it as a tool that has multiple uses. For example, a hammer can be used to hammer nails into a board and help with construction, but when presented in the wrong way, it could be used to inflict real damage on a building or even a person.

So if we were to look at our beliefs as tools, we might realize that a negative belief could actually be shaped to be helpful to us instead of continuing this damage. For example, if you have a negative belief that leads you to live a very shy and closed off life, you could discover humility, strength of character and the ability to be alone are all good components out of that negative belief. You can then change the negative belief into a positive one and take all of the good things out of it.

Figuring out what the opposite of a negative belief isn't necessarily easy, but once you have an idea of what it looks like, it's time to move onto the next step.

Positive Belief Step Three: Frame the Positive Belief in Healthy Language.

Okay, let's suppose that you are working to change your self-worth belief. You might be tempted to frame it in the context of a negative, you could say "I'm not a worthless person!" And you could mean that with every fiber of your being, but it wouldn't work very well. Do you know why? Because you framed your positive belief in negative language. The brain doesn't have the ability to turn the concept of not worthless into something positive, so it instead focused on the worthless feelings that you are trying to avoid and it will then inform you that you are a worthless person.

Instead, always frame your positive beliefs in healthy language that is positive. Don't speak in the context of not, instead focus entirely on the context of *is*. For example, instead of saying "I'm not worthless," try saying "I am inherently a valuable person" or "I have worth." These words not only change our inner thoughts, but it will also allow you to hold onto a positive affirmation to give yourself on a daily basis.

Positive Belief Step Four: Make Sure Your Belief Is Internally Driven

There can be a tremendous temptation to attach our new positive beliefs to external qualifiers. A qualifier is something like "Because I am so good at sports, I have value." These kinds of things might sound good, but they aren't healthy due to the fact that they are built on an external fact. You don't need to use any kind of justification or qualification in order to get your brain to develop a new belief, because the brain isn't interested in using logic to determine your internal reality. Your brain develops new beliefs entirely based on what you are thinking at all times, so when you try to attach an external qualifier to your new belief, you are essentially shooting yourself in the foot. There will be a time when you aren't good at sports, or you might injure yourself, or things might change on you drastically. If you have created a positive belief that is contingent on some kind of external circumstances being favorable, you are setting yourself up for an eventual failure.

Not only are you setting yourself up to fail, but you are also doing so needlessly. The brain has little to no interest in reality, so attaching your beliefs to external realities don't really matter.

**Positive Belief Step Five: Develop
strong self-talk**

If there is a single crucial element to
developing a new belief, it lies within how you
communicate to yourself internally. Everyone
speaks to themselves in their own heads, it is one
of the most natural things that you could
possibly do. Since we have a habit of always
communicating to ourselves, making comments
about our actions, how we feel about ourselves,
how we look, etc., we must be conscious with
how we talk to ourselves.

Up until the point where you start to
develop positive voices, you might find that the
Inner Critic has been the primary method of
communication with yourself for most of your
life. You look in the mirror and the inner critic

tells you that you are ugly. You do a project and the inner critic tells you that you did a bad job. Your self-talk at this point is unhealthy and extremely destructive to yourself. But now we're reaching a point where you are starting to develop new ways of thinking as well as new beliefs. If you do not learn how to get a grip on your self-talk, however, you will find that most of your new ways of thinking won't stick around.

The first thing to bring up is that we must stop looking at negative self-talk as intrusive, unwanted thoughts that arrive out of nowhere. Instead, we must look at them as simply the results of an old habit, an old way of thinking. By choosing to develop a new, positive belief, you are walking away from your old habit and as such, you must build up a new habit. Don't try to

83

counter your negative self-talk, because that gives it credit and allows it to have a voice at the table. Instead, just simply acknowledge that the thought exists and let it go on its way.

We don't have to believe every thought that comes into our mind. The human brain is a powerful machine and it generates a great many thoughts in a single moment. Some of these thoughts can be outright weird or bizarre. For example, if you were standing near a ledge, looking at a beautiful view, you might feel a sudden urge to leap. This urge is just an intrusive thought and it's your brains method of trying to warn you about the dangers by bringing the entire scenario to your mind. You might nervously take a step back, but you aren't honestly going to jump just because your brain brought this image to your mind, would you? These intrusive thoughts are here quickly and gone the next, and they have no control over what we do with our lives.

Just like you don't have to listen to an intrusive thought that tells you to do something stupid or dangerous, you also don't have to listen to negative self-talk. When it arrives, acknowledge it and then let it go. Don't try to argue or fight with it, don't counter it. Treat it like you would an anonymous commenter on the internet who's point is invalid and frustration to you. If you try to fight against the commenter, he's just going to provoke you into fighting more. If you read him comment and keep scrolling, you'll never have to worry about him again.

Once you get to the place where you are able to allow negative self-talk to pass through your mind without being held onto, you can then begin to focus on proactively developing your own positive self-talk. Anytime you find yourself talking to yourself, try to focus on being as constructive as possible instead of being destructive. For example, let's suppose that you were trying on clothes and in the mirror, you were trying to judge how you looked. The negative voice would say something like "You aren't very good looking and that outfit is ugly on you." Now, you might not actually like the outfit but that doesn't mean that your criticism should be so brutal. Instead, you could say something like "This outfit doesn't work for me, I don't like it."

It's important that as we begin to develop positive self-talk that we learn how to separate judgments from evaluations. A judgment is a harsh pronouncement about how things are. For example, if you said to yourself "you are so stupid" that would be a judgment on yourself. Those words sink in deep into your subconscious mind and settle down, working to reinforce the old beliefs and supplant the new ones. An evaluation, however, is a valid piece of criticism without the emotional impact behind it. For example, if you said "You said something stupid to your friend" that isn't an emotional phrase because it is focusing on evaluating what has happened. This doesn't affect your brain nearly as badly as a judgment and won't serve to reinforce negative thoughts.

The difference between judgment and evaluation lies in who is the target of the phrase. Judgment statements target you, evaluations target your actions. Everyone knows that we are not our actions, there is far more to who we are than what we do. So evaluations are far more fair and healthy than judgments, which can only stand to condemn ourselves. It is very easy to fall into the judgment trap, because we usually feel vindicated on some level. There is usually some kind of evidence that we are able to find that will dictate how we judge ourselves.

The problem is this evidence is usually from our own negative perspective. For example, let's suppose you made a dumb joke and no one found it funny, so an hour later you're still kicking yourself over it and telling yourself how dumb you are and how unfunny you are because of that joke. You are judging based on the "evidence" but the evidence is really that no one else laughed at a joke you made. Was it a period of awkwardness? Sure. But that is hardly reason for you should come down so hard on yourself, after all, you were making plenty of jokes earlier and everyone was laughing. Why do 100 funny jokes get ignored when it comes to submitting evidence, yet the one time you did mess up condemns you? This is because those judgmental types of self-talks are fueled by our negative beliefs about ourselves. This is why we learn to make the transition from judgment to evaluation. So you no longer say to yourself 'You aren't funny" and instead say "Wow that joke really wasn't funny."

Positive Belief Step Six: Visualize Change

The last and most important part of changing your beliefs from a negative to positive is to develop a strong vision of what the future looks like for you. There is a lot of work required in order to change your habits, because our thinking tends to be very automatic once our beliefs have been formed. The process of changing from having unconscious thoughts runs our lives to living a very intentional and conscious life is a difficult change. We aren't allowed to simply let our automatic thinking control us anymore, because our automatic thinking will be sabotaging our efforts.

The word we would use to describe how we will think from this point on is "intentionality." You must be intentionally working toward developing new habits and methods of thinking. This requires you to be on your toes at all times. While we would like to just set up a new belief and allow it to completely change the way we think, we don't really have that kind of luxury. Instead, it takes work. However, you will find that over time, the more effort and energy that you have into focusing on changing the way you think, the less maintenance and energy that it will take in the long run. The process of transitioning a habit from being a conscious, measured effort to being automatic takes time, but it does happen. Eventually your thinking will change from being an effort to a habit. Usually this takes somewhere around 66 to 80 days or so. But once you have that habit ingrained into your personality, your new belief will be far easier to maintain.

Even though it will be easy at some point in the future, we must recognize that when you first start off, it will be a tremendous expenditure of energy. Not only will it take energy to start, but building a new belief will take energy to maintain. How then, can we stay consistently motivated to continue working towards healing our minds and building ourselves to be the person that we've always wanted to be? It is quite simple: you must be willing to build a strong enough vision so that you are inspired to push through the discomfort of changing the way you think.

The stronger your vision for the end is, the harder you will work in the tougher times. This means that you must be willing to visualize what a life of freedom from your negative thoughts would look like. The power of visualization also helps your brain begin to grow and change as well. Studies have shown that the ability to visualize about the future in specific instances can actually help the brain respond when it is time to perform. For example, if an athlete visualizes performance in a sporting event, he will actually perform better than an athlete who doesn't use visualization. Why is that? Because the brain doesn't have a good handle on the difference between fantasy and reality, the more you think about something in the future, the more your brain will be convinced that it is already happening. This is helpful when it comes to positive development, because if your brain is able to anticipate positive change and growth, it will fight against you less as you begin to change. This reduces the amount of energy that you have to spend and speeds up the entire process of developing a new pattern of belief.

Once you have made it through all of these steps, you will find that you will have a much richer inner life. It's not an easy process to go through the process of examination, deconstruction and then rebuilding, but in doing so, you are making your life far better!

Chapter 5: Conclusion

The nature of the human mind is to stay where it is. There are always going to be reasons inside of your mind as to why you should keep your habits and beliefs. The hardest change that can ever happen in a human being is when they make the conscious decision to change the way they think. There is tremendous pressure on us from both inside of our minds and even outside of our minds. When we think one way, we tend to surround ourselves with people who also think like us. These support systems can be extremely unhealthy and will actually drag us down when we begin to change.

As you begin your journey, to find true transformation, you might want to look at the voices and influences around you and ask if they are really healthy for you. If you have people who are able to cheer you on and assist you in your plans to renew the way you think, then you will be successful, but if you are surrounded by people who only echo the darkness inside of you, then you will found yourself dragged down to the ground. We are usually only as healthy as our support systems will allow. The act of change is a hard thing to do and with people who are actively working against you, you might find yourself growing very weary. Make the right decision and find people who will help you become the best version of you possible. When you make this choice, you will quickly discover how much easier it is to form new beliefs.

The process of change is possible for anyone who is willing to endure the hard road to get there. It isn't easy, it's not fun, but when you are able to overcome these negative beliefs and grow beautiful, positives thoughts, you will know it was all worth it.

Other books available by Landon T. Smith on Kindle, paperback and audio:

Why NLP Isn't Working For You

The Art of Influence

The Power of Reflection: Embrace Your Past to Find a Purpose for Your Future

Meet Maslow: How Understanding the Priorities of Those Around Us Can Lead to Harmony and Improvement

Manderstanding: Learn How to Read the Cues
and Understand the Motives of the Male Gender

The End of Chaos: Break Away From Bad Habits,
Addictions and Self Destructive Tendencies
Before They Break You